D0332214

The
Body of Christ:
A Reality

WATCHMAN NEE

Translated from the Chinese

Christian Fellowship Publishers, Inc.
New York

Copyright © 1978
Christian Fellowship Publishers, Inc.
New York
All Rights Reserved
ISBN 0-935008-13-6

Available from the Publishers at:

11515 Allecingie Parkway
Richmond, Virginia 23235

PRINTED IN U.S.A.

TRANSLATOR'S PREFACE

"And gave him [Christ] to be head over all things to the church, which is his body, the fulness of him that filleth all in all" (Eph. 1.22, 23). As Christ the head is a reality, so the church as the body of Christ is a reality. To many, however, the body of Christ is a vague, nebulous and abstract term. It is merely a beautiful concept or a noble theory. It is not a living reality as is presented in the Scriptures. The time has come, and now is, that all who seek the Lord should enter into a new understanding of the body of Christ. We need to see that the body of Christ is a life which we live in. It ought to become our daily experience.

In this little volume of collected messages selected for the unity of their subject matter and given by the author through years of faithful ministry, Watchman Nee attempts to show us the reality of the body of Christ. He proves to us that the body of Christ is founded on life and life consciousness. It is built on a living relationship among its members as well as with its head. This body is governed by its own laws, and blessed are those who discover these laws and follow them. To them the body of Christ is indeed a living reality.

May God grant to all who read this book wisdom and strength for living in the reality of the body of Christ.

CONTENTS

Translator's Preface   *v*

1 Life and Consciousness   1

2 The Consciousness of the Body of Christ   9

3 Hold Fast the Head   23

4 The Service of the Member   33

5 The Function and Harmony of the Members   43

6 Obeying the Law of the Body of Christ   51

7 The Covering, Restraint, and Supply of the
   Body of Christ   71

8 Three Cardinal Principles on Living in the
   Body of Christ   85

Scripture quotations are from the
American Standard Version
of the Bible (1901),
unless otherwise indicated.

1 | Life and Consciousness

In Him was life; and the life was the light of men. (John 1.4)

So then, brethren, we are debtors, not to the flesh, to live after the flesh. (Rom. 8.12)

And whether one member suffereth, all the members suffer with it; or one member is honored, all the members rejoice with it. (1Cor. 12.26)

From the human standpoint, life seems to be rather intangible and quite abstract. How can anyone present life in such manner as to cause people to recognize that it in fact is life? We cannot take life as such and explain it to others, neither can others explain it to us. Nevertheless, we may all know and recognize this life through the feeling of life's consciousness, which to us is far more substantial. Now by the same token, the life which God has given to the Christian believer can likewise be known by its consciousness. Although we cannot take hold of such divine life and show it to ourselves or to other people, we nonetheless know we have this *new* life because there is within us an altogether *new* consciousness.

Consciousness of God's Life

After a person has accepted the Lord we say he not only is saved but also has been regenerated. This means that this man is now born of God. He has received a new life from Him. Yet this is something difficult to explain. How does he know he has the life of God? How will other people know he has divine life? How will the church recognize that he has the life of God? The presence of divine life is proven through life's consciousness. If the life of God is in him, the consciousness of that life must be in him as well.

What is life's consciousness? A Christian who is occasionally overcome by sin feels most uncomfortable. And this is one facet of consciousness. He feels restless when he sins. He immediately senses a veil between him and God after he has sinned and instantly loses his inner joy. Such manifestations as these are facets of life's consciousness, for because the life of God hates sin, therefore a person who has God's life must also have a certain feeling against sin. The very fact of his possessing this life's sense proves he possesses such life.

Suppose a man says he has confessed he is a sinner and has also accepted the Lord Jesus as his Savior, but he never has any sense against sin. Is this man born again? In such a case, if he should commit any sin, someone has to go to his home and tell him that what he has done is wrong before he will ever acknowledge that he has indeed done wrong. When a person asks him why he commits such a wrong, he will ignorantly answer, Why can't I do it? When a second time he is informed that he has committed another sin, he again will confess he has done something wrong. Yet not long afterwards he commits another sin, and someone is once more obliged to tell him of this transgression before he once again acknowledges his wrong. Here, it is not that he does not listen to his prompter's word; as a matter of fact he is quite obedient to the other person's word. The problem is, though, that he himself has no spiritual consciousness. Can it therefore be said that such a person has God's life if he is utterly void of any spiritual awareness and that others have to feel for him? If he has the life of God, he should have its consciousness within him. It is absolutely impossible for a person to have spiritual life and yet not have the consciousness of that life. The life of God is not somthing nebulous, nor is it abstract; it is very concrete and substantial. And how do we know it is substantial? Because such life has its own consciousness.

Having the life of God, a person is not only, negatively speaking, aware of sins but he also, positively speaking, knows God: for what we receive is not the spirit of a bond-slave but the spirit of sonship. We just naturally feel that God is very approachable and that calling Him "Abba, Father" is most sweet (Gal. 4.6). The Holy Spirit bears witness with our spirit that we are children of God (Rom. 8.16). Knowing God as

Father is therefore the inner consciousness of this life.

Some people merely have doctrinal understanding; they have never met God; and they are therefore afraid of Him whom they cannot touch. They do not have any life relationship with God, and the Holy Spirit has not borne witness with their spirit that they are God's children. They cannot cry out of their spirit, Abba, Father. Such people may pray, though in their prayer they neither sense the distance of sin nor the nearness of the Lord. They do not have the feeling of the awfulness of sin nor the intimacy of God. They have no relationship with Him because they have not yet received new life from Him. Hence they do not feel that God is near, nor do they sense that Christ has already removed the wall of partition between them and God. In short, they do not have the consciousness of being the children of God. They may confess that they are Christians, but their feeling before God is inadequate. Though with their mouth they may say, "Heavenly Father", there is no such sensation within them. Only the presence of such a consciousness proves the existence of such a life. Now if there has never been such an awareness, how can anyone say that there is such life within them?

Body Consciousness a Facet of Life's Consciousness

The same is true with regard to the body of Christ. Many brothers and sisters ask: How can I say I have seen the body of Christ? On what ground may I assert that I have lived out the life of the body of Christ? Our answer is simple: all who know the life of the body of Christ will have the consciousness of the body of Christ. If you have really seen the body, you cannot but have body consciousness—because the life in you being a reality and an experience, it cannot fail to show forth its consciousness. You perceive the body of Christ not only as a principle or as a teaching but you discover that the body of Christ is a matter of real inward consciousness.

"And whether one member suffereth, all the members suffer with it; or one member is honored, all the members rejoice with it" (1 Cor. 12.26). Suffering is a sensation, so is rejoicing a sensation. Although the members are many, the life is one, and so, too, the consciousness is one.

Let us take the example of a person who may have had installed in his body an artificial leg. Now although it may appear to be almost the same as the other real leg, it nevertheless has no life in it. It therefore has no body consciousness; for when other members suffer, this artificial leg does not feel anything—when other members rejoice, the artificial limb senses no elation. All the other members have the same awareness because they all possess the one common life. The artificial leg alone has no awareness because there is not that life in it.

Life cannot be simulated, nor does it need to be. If there is life there is no need to pretend; if there is not life there is no possibility to pretend. The most distinctive expression of life is its consciousness. Hence a Christian who sees the body life will invariably have body consciousness with other members of the body.

The Teaching of the Body v. Its Reality

In spiritual things, knowing doctrine without having consciousness is of no avail. Someone, for instance, may say that lying is a sin which he should not commit because he has been told by other people that a Christian should not tell lies. The real issue here is not a matter of whether or not it is right to lie, rather is it a question of whether he is inwardly aware of it or not when he tells a lie. If he has no inward consciousness that his lying is sin, then however much he may confess with his mouth that lying is a sin, it does not help him at all. He may say on the one hand that a person should not lie but on the other hand he constantly lies. What is special with those who have God's life is that when they lie outwardly, they feel bad inwardly—not because they know doctrinally that lying is wrong, but because they feel uncomfortable inwardly if they do lie. This is what being called a Christian really signifies. What characterizes a Christian is an inward awareness of this life consciousness of which we have been speaking. He who has no life and no inner consciousness is not a Christian. Outward rules are merely standards, not life.

Let it be said that it is totally inadequate for a person to say, "I know the teaching of the body of Christ, therefore I must not move independently"; he needs also to have an inner consciousness of such a teaching. Suppose he says with his mouth that he should not be independent and yet when he acts independently he fails to be aware of such independence; he is thereby proven to have never truly seen the body of Christ.

This does not mean he has not heard the teaching of the body of Christ: it simply indicates that he has not seen its reality.

Hearing the teaching and seeing the reality of the body of Christ belong to two totally different realms. Hearing the teaching of the body is merely an outward understanding of a principle, whereas seeing the body of Christ produces a consciousness within. It is similar to the situation in which merely hearing the doctrine of salvation only gives the person the knowledge of how God saves sinners, but that inwardly accepting the Lord Jesus as Savior creates within that person an awareness of God as well as a consciousness of sin. What a difference between the two! Consequently, we should not overlook this matter of life consciousness (it not simply being an outward sensation, but an inward feeling too). Such consciousness is life's expression. The presence or absence of this consciousness reveals the reality or unreality within. It gives us insight into whether or not there is the life of Christ within.

Life's consciousness is distinctive in that it enables you to know spontaneously without the need of being told. It is too late if you must be told before you know. What would happen if every Christian needed to be told what sin is and what should not be done? What if, in this event, nobody is at your side? What if you forget after being told? Oh, let us see that a Christian does not act according to what he hears from people without, but he is motivated by what he is told from within. Within him is a life—an inner light, an inner consciousness. It comes from the inner shining of

God's light: it comes from the life inside and not from outside information.

When we are born again we receive a very real life. We thus have within us a very real consciousness. The reality of such consciousness proves the reality of divine life. Let us ask God to be merciful to us that we may always touch this life consciousness and live therein. Let us also ask God to give us rich consciousness so that we may have a sensitive awareness in all things: that we may be aware of God, of sin, of the body of Christ, and of all spiritual realities. May God lead our way and glorify His own name!

2 | The Consciousness of the Body of Christ

> For I say, through the grace that was given me, to every man that is among you, not to think of himself more highly than he ought to think; but so to think soberly, according as God hath dealt to each man a measure of faith. For even as we have many members in one body, and all the members have not the same office: so we, who are many, are one body in Christ, and severally members one of another. (Rom. 12.3–5)

In the previous chapter we came to understand a little how consciousness reveals life. Here we will continue further so that we may understand what the consciousness of the body of Christ exactly is.

Love the Brethren

Let us first approach it from the standpoint of love. One thing is quite marvelous when we contemplate this verse: "We know that we have passed out of death into life, because we love the brethren" (1 John 3.14). All who have passed out of death into life love one another. All who have become members of the

same spiritual body love one another. Such love comes
from life and it flows spontaneously. Could a person
be considered a child of God if, after answering af-
firmatively in a church meeting that he is a Christian
and after being reminded that as a Christian he ought
to love other Christians, he then says, "I will start to
love other Christians tomorrow if you say so"? Oh let
us see that everyone who is truly born from above and
has the life of God spontaneously loves all who are
members together with him in the body of Christ.
Whether he is reminded or not, he has a consciousness
of loving the brethren. He unquestionably needs many
times to be reminded of loving the brethren. Yet this
reminder does not add anything to him which is not
already within him, it instead merely stirs up into
more fervency what is already present in him. If the
love of God is present in a person, the love of the
brethren is there. And if God's love is absent, broth-
erly love is not there. It is that simple. Nothing can be
created or manufactured. When a believer meets another person who belongs to God he strangely but
quite naturally loves him because he has that inner
consciousness within him which must express itself in
love towards that other person.

Once a son was born to a brother in Christ. He
was asked, "Now that you have become a father, do
you love your son?" His answer was: "A week before I
was to be a father, I kept thinking how I should love
my son. But as soon as my son was born—the moment
I saw him—my heart quite naturally went out to him
and I simply loved him." We see here how human love
springs from a consciousness inside, it is not taught

from outside. Likewise, all the children of God who are bought with the blood of the Lamb and receive God's life and are baptized into the body of Christ cannot help but be moved from within to love one another as members of the same body.

Oftentimes when you meet an individual who is truly of the Lord, your heart goes out to him as soon as you learn he is a Christian, regardless whether he comes from abroad or is a native citizen, whether he is highly civilized or uncultured, or regardless of what race or profession he may be. Love is an inner consciousness. If you are in the same spiritual body, you naturally have this kind of consciousness.

No Division

One who has seen the body of Christ and who thus possesses the consciousness of the body feels unbearable inside when he does anything which may cause division or separate God's children. For he loves all who belong to God and cannot divide His children. Love is natural to the body of Christ, whereas division is most unnatural. It is just as in the case with our two hands: no matter for how many reasons one hand may be raised against the other hand, there is no way to sever their relationship: division is simply impossible.

Perhaps a person is proud of himself for being one who has left a sect and thus deems himself to be a person who knows the body of Christ. As a matter of fact, however, leaving a denomination is not necessarily the same as, or an indication of, seeing the body of Christ. It is quite true that whoever discerns the body is deliv-

ered from denominationalism. But who can claim he
has apprehended the body of Christ simply because he
has left a denomination? Outwardly many have left a
denomination, yet they simply set up another kind for
themselves elsewhere. Their leaving the denomination
merely demonstrates their own latent feeling of supe-
riority; they fail to comprehend that all the members
of the body are their brothers and sisters and therefore
all are loving. For this reason, let us realize that all
sectarian spirit, divisive attitude, outward action, or
inward thought which separate God's children are the
unfailing signs of not knowing the body of Christ.

The body of Christ will deliver us from sect and
sectarianism; it will also save us from self and individualism. How sad that the life principle of many is
not the body but the individual self. We may discover
this principle of individualism in many areas. For example, in a prayer meeting someone can only pray by
himself, since he cannot pray with other people. His
physical body may kneel together with others, yet his
consciousness is circumscribed by his own self. When
he prays, he wishes other people to listen to him; but
when *others* pray, he will not listen to them. He has
no inner response to another's prayer, and he is unable
even to offer up an amen. His consciousness is disconnected from the consciousness of other people. Hence
he prays *his* prayers and lets the others pray *their*
prayers. There appears to be no relationship between
his prayers and those of the others. When he comes to
the meeting he seems to do so only for the sake of ut-
tering whatever words are pent up within him, and
thereafter feels that his job is done. He does not care

what prayer burden or consciousness others present may have. This is the rule of individualism, not the principle of the body. In point of fact he has not seen the body, and thus he cannot cooperate with other people before God.

Sometimes three or five, even ten or twenty brethren at a meeting will all speak only whatever concerns themselves, without showing any interest in the affairs of the others or listening to the others' thoughts. Or, as the case might be, as you or others sit with such a person as has been described, he may talk with animation for an hour or two about his own business; but when you or the others talk, he does not pay the slightest attention—for if you ask him afterwards, he evidences the fact that he hardly seems to have heard anything. In small things such as these, you can tell if a person has truly discerned the body of Christ.

The plague of individualism can grow from simply expressing one person's individualism to that of several persons. You may notice in the church that three or five, perhaps even eight or nine persons will sometimes form a small circle. Only these few are of one mind and love one another. They do not fit in with the other brothers and sisters. This indicates that they too have not perceived the body of Christ. The church is one, it cannot be severed. If a person has really known the body, he cannot endorse any kind of individualism. He cannot form a party or any small circle.

If you have genuinely experienced the body of Christ you will be conscious of something wrong whenever you begin to show your individualism, and obviously you dare not take any action. Or else, when you or several others should make a wrong move, this body consciousness will cause you to be aware of being disconnected from the other children of God, thus preventing you from proceeding further. There is something in you which restrains, speaks, reproves, warns, or hinders. This consciousness of life can deliver all of us from any taint of division.

Deliver from Independent Work

If we have body consciousness we will comprehend immediately that the body is one. Thus, in spiritual work, it cannot be individualistic in its scope. In order to participate rightly in the Lord's work, it is imperative that we deal with this matter of independent labor. In the thinking of some people, a person must lay his own hand on things or else that person will consider those things to be good for nothing. Whatever is done by *him* is deemed as having spiritual value; what is not done by him has no value at all. When he preaches and nobody is saved, he feels depressed. When he preaches and people are saved, he shows pleasant surprise. This is because he looks at the work as his own personal labor. But the moment God's children preceive the oneness of the body, they immediately comprehend the oneness of the work. The instant they see that the body is one, they are delivered from their individual endeavor since they now see the work of the body. This does not imply that a person can no longer labor as an individual. It simply means that he can no longer consider work as belonging solely to himself. Whether the work is done by him or not is no problem anymore, so long as it is done by someone.

As Christians, we should admire and seek for spiritual things, but we ought not have any emulative pretensions nor any trace of jealousy. Our attitude individually towards spiritual work should be: What I can do I hope others can also do; and what I cannot do I wish someone else can do; I would like to do more as well as I would expect other people to do more. How I need to realize that I can only be a single vessel in the work; I cannot monopolize it. I dare not consider the work and its result as altogether mine. If I insist that everything must be done by me, I have not apprehended the body. The moment I apprehend the body, immediately I realize that both my labor and that of others mean gain to the head as well as to the body. And let all glory be to the Lord and all blessings be to the church.

The Lord distributes His work to all, and everyone has his share. We must not think of ourselves more highly than we ought to think. We should be faithful to the portion which the Lord has given each of us; but we should also respect the portion He gives to others. Many young people possess a kind of competitive attitude in which they are always comparing what they have with that which others do not have and what they do not have with that which others have. Actually, such comparison is absurd. How can we add a chair to a table? Are they one or two? A table plus a chair equals a table and a chair. If we are asked which is better, the hand or the eye, we can only answer that the hand and the eye are both good. He who has seen the body recognizes the functions of all the members. He looks at himself as only one among many members. He will not project himself to a distinctive position in order to compare himself favorably with others or even to occupy another's place.

As soon as a Christian inwardly discerns the body of Christ he has no way or justification to be either proud or jealous. Since the body is one, it makes no difference whether the work is done by him or by others. Whether by him or by other people, all glory goes to the Lord and all blessings flow to the church. If anyone sees the body of Christ, there will naturally be within him this consciousness: that the body is one, and therefore the work is one.

See the Need for Fellowship

He who sees the body of Christ most spontaneously sees not only the stupidity of independent action but the need for fellowship as well. Fellowship is not an external exercise in social intercourse; it is the spontaneous demand of body life. What is erroneously but commonly assumed to be fellowship by God's children is a visiting of homes of some brothers and sisters at times of leisure and chit-chatting with them a while. In actuality, fellowship means realizing the total inadequacy of my own self. I am desirous of doing all things with the other members of the body. Although for doing many things I am not able to gather all the brothers and sisters in the church, I still can do them with two or three brothers and/or sisters according to the principle of the body.

Oftentimes we need to learn fellowship in prayer, to learn fellowship in difficulties, to learn fellowship in seeking God's will, to learn fellowship concerning our future, and to learn fellowship regarding God's word. What fellowship means is that, knowing that I am inadequate in the matter of prayer, I seek out two or three others to pray with me. I by myself am incompetent in solving difficulties, hence I ask two or three brethren to deal with the situations together with me. Alone I am unable to know God's will, therefore I solicit the help of two or three others. I in myself am rather confused as to my future, consequently I request two or three brothers and sisters to fellowship and decide with me what my future should be. I cannot understand God's word alone, so now I study the word of God with two or three brothers and sisters. In fellowship, I acknowledge my insufficiency and incompetency, and I also acknowledge my need of the body. I confess that I am limited and liable to make mistakes; for this I plead with those brothers and sisters who have spiritual discernment to help me (and not just ask those to help me who are affectionate towards me). I am inadequate, and hence I need the help of other brethren.

The body of Christ is a life, and there is therefore also a consciousness involved. You yourself will become conscious or aware of the fact that without fellowship you cannot live.

Learn to Be a Member

If a person has body consciousness he at once

recognizes his place in the body; that is to say, he sees himself as being one of its members. Each member has his distinctive usefulness. A member of a physical body is different from a body cell. Lacking a cell does not matter much, but the lack of a member in a body is unthinkable. Of course, a cell has its use, but please note that the Bible in its use of the analogy of the human body says that we are *members* of the body of Christ, not cells. How pitiful that the conditions of many Christians are like those of cells in the human body instead of members. Such a person seems to have no specific use in the body of Christ, neither does he fulfill his part. In any given church meeting his presence does not appear to add anything to the body of Christ, and his absence does not give the appearance to the body that it is lacking in anything. He has not discharged his function in the body because he has never seen the body. When he is with brothers and sisters he never knows his ministry, neither does he even realize what he should do. Were he to perceive the body he could not help but see himself as a member. Were he to perceive the body, he would know that it will suffer loss if he does not supply life to it.

No one can be passive in a meeting. Each person is a member of the body, and consequently no one can come to a meeting as a passive spectator. As we gather together we pray because we realize we are mutual members of the body of Christ. Whether uttered or unuttered, we nonetheless pray, for we want to supply life to the body.

Some Christians are life-supplying members. When they attend a meeting, even if they do not open their mouths, their very presence lifts the meeting; for they are there supplying life, they are there swallowing up death. Once anyone discerns the body of Christ, he cannot fail to recognize himself as a member of the body.

Because we are members of the body of Christ and members each in its part, we must seek how to help the body in gaining life and strength. In any gathering, even if we do not open our mouths, we may pray silently. Even though we may not speak, we can still look to God. This is body consciousness. If we have seen the body, we cannot say we are a person of no consequence. We will rather say: I am a member of the body, and hence I have a duty to perform. I have a word which I should speak, I have a prayer which I should utter. When I come to the meeting I must do whatever God wants me to do. I cannot afford to be a spectator. Such things as these are what we will say or do if we truly apprehend the body. And as we all function, the life of the entire gathering will swallow up all death. Many meetings fail to exhibit such power to overcome death for there are too many spectators.

Submit to Authority

If you really see the body of Christ you are conscious of the loveliness of God's children, of the error of division, of the need for fellowship, and of the responsibility in you as a member of the body of Christ. All these facets of awareness are because of body consciousness. Moreover, as you are aware that you are in the body, you must become equally aware that you are

under the authority of the head. For whoever knows
the life of the body of Christ and is conscious of being
a body member will invariably sense the authority of
the head, who is Christ Jesus the Lord.

We must not only submit to the *direct* authority of
the head, we need also to submit to the *indirect*
authority of the head. My physical hand is under the
direct authority of the head of my body, but when my
arm moves, my hand moves together with my arm—
for my hand submits to the head through the arm.
Consequently, whoever sees the body of Christ sees
also the authority which God has set in the body of
Christ for him to submit to.

Sometimes when you are told by someone in the
church to do a certain thing, you do not sense it is the
Lord's will for you after you have prayed about it.
And so you do not do it, and you feel happy. You
know it is right for you to listen to the Lord's word
rather than to man's word. On the other hand, is there
an instance when you become aware that if you do not
listen to your brother or sister you come into conflict
with the Lord? Is there one time, or even a number of
times, wherein you have the sense that one or more of
the brethren who know the Lord have been placed by
Him in the position of representing His authority and
that if you enter into controversy with them you are in
controversy with the Lord? If you truly perceive the
authority of the head, you will also perceive that one
or more members of the body are ahead of you, and
that to them you must learn to submit. Hence you
recognize not only the head but also those whom God
has set in the body to represent the head. If you are at

odds with them, you will also be at odds with God.

If our eyes have been opened by the Lord to recognize the body, we will also recognize authority. When we behold the human body, why is it that all parts work so harmoniously as to reveal the fact that the entire body is one? This is because there is authority in the body. If there is no authority the entire body will be thrown into confusion. Suppose, for example, that the stomach is hungry for food, but that the mouth refuses to eat; what will happen to that man? The entire body will suffer if but one of its parts refuses to obey its authority. Or again, take the example of cancer, which we know is a most serious disease. How does cancer arise in the body? It is due to a few cells which develop themselves independently and not according to the law of the body. The body does not require them to develop in such a way, yet they insist on growing abnormally. They absorb many useful nutrients by which to supply their own growth. They only mind their own development: they do not care if the body does not need such growth: they do not obey the authority of the body but act independently on their own. Now the larger they grow, the more damage the body incurs. With the result that a few insubordinate cells may cause death to the entire body.

It is clear from the above observations that authority is the law of the human body, and insubordination to it is symptomatic of disease in the body. Equally true will this be in the spiritual body of Christ. If a person does not know what authority is, how can he say he knows the body of Christ? Let us see that the one who knows the body can discern—even when only three or five people are assembled together—who among those assembled is his authority; because there is manifested in their midst the authority of the head to which he needs to submit. How natural and how beautiful it is in the human body for the fingers to submit to the wrist, the wrist to the arm, the arm to the shoulder, and so on. And this same beauty can be displayed in the body of Christ.

Certain Christians are so careless in action as well as in speech that they will not listen to anyone. They seem to regard themselves as being the greatest to such an extent that they fail to recognize anyone to whom they could submit. This proves that such believers have never known the restraint of the body nor have ever submitted to the authority of the head. May God have mercy on such members. If we have genuinely been dealt with by the Lord and if our flesh has received such dealings as to have had the backbone of the natural life broken, we will immediately acknowledge how neither our hands nor our mouth have unlimited freedom—since all are under the control of the body—and how we cannot fail to submit ourselves to the authority which God has set in the body of Christ.

May we not remain merely in the realm of teaching on this matter, but be truly led of God to know and to experience the body of Christ. May this body consciousness in its many facets always follow us so that we have no way to do anything according to our own will, or to live carelessly through our days. Thus shall we receive rich supply through this body, and we will be able to manifest the testimony of the Lord.

3 | Hold Fast the Head

And he put all things in subjection under his feet, and gave him to be head over all things to the church. (Eph. 1.22)

But speaking truth in love, may grow up in all things into him, who is the head, even Christ; from whom all the body fitly framed and knit together through that which every joint supplieth, according to the working in due measure of each several part, maketh the increase of the body unto the building up of itself in love. (Eph. 4.15–16)

And not holding fast the head, from whom all the body, being supplied and knit together through the joints and bands, increaseth with the increase of God. (Col. 2.19)

One

In order to make Christ the head of all things, God first made Him the head of the church. After being made the head of the church, Christ will later have

His authority extended to be head over all things. His future position in the universe is closely related to His place today in the church. For Christ to be head over all things, God wants Him first to be such among His children—that is, in the church which is His body. How exceedingly important a subject is this matter.

Christ being the head of the church and the church being the body of Christ, the whole body is thus summed up in the head. Nothing in the body can live outside of the head. If our human body is separated from the head, that automatically means death to our body. All the movements of a person are governed by the head. Whenever the head is wounded and thereby loses its effectiveness, the activities of the body stop and the body ends in death; for the head is the central control of the life of the body. Now the word of God declares that he who has the Son of God has life (1 John 5.12). A Christian receives life from the Lord Jesus, who is the Son of God; yet this life never leaves the Lord. He who has the Son has life, but this life, says God's word, is in the Son (1 John 5.11), and not even for a moment has this life left the Son. Hence, apart from the Lord Jesus we just cannot live.

Let us understand that God has not apportioned to us a small amount of Christ so that we may take that portion and go away. No, God has given the total Christ to us and has joined us intimately with His Son. All the power of our existence rests in Christ. In the event we lose communication with the Lord because we have departed from Him, we instantly become lifeless. Thus, though a Christian receives life from Christ, it remains in the Lord. We have received life, yet this life and the head are inseparable. Upon our accepting Him, we still must live in Him. Though we have received Him, we are yet to depend on Him. Accordingly, we cannot be independent in anything. The Lord alone is head, and He is the sole resource of our life.

Two

Christ is the life of the body; He also is its authority as the head. Because life is in Him, authority too is in Him. He is our life, therefore He has authority; and when we obey His authority, we have life. Hence if we see what is the body of Christ, we cannot avoid accepting the control of the head, since a body with its members is not able to move at will but does so only at the order of the head. If there is no command from the head there is no movement in the body. No member of the body can take its own initiative, but must be governed by the head. Where life is, there is authority. True authority is life. And since the Lord controls our life, He has authority over us.

Anyone who confesses with his mouth that he knows body life ought to ask himself if he has subjected himself to the Lord's authority. Whether or not he is in subjection to the authority of the head proves whether or not he really knows the life of the body. The attitude of some people to the word of God is: "This is what the Lord has indeed said, but I think . . ." Who allows any of us to say "But"? Who gives us such an authority to say "But"? In the world, if anyone does not follow the order of his superior he is deemed an insubordinate person. Since Christ is the head and we are not, we have no right not to obey the Lord.

What is meant by "follow"? To follow signifies that the way I tread and the place where I go are all decided by someone else. We are following the Lord; therefore we have no authority to decide our own path. The body in its relation to the head can only obey and follow. If we wish to live out the life of the body of Christ we must cover our own head; that is to say, we must not have our personal opinion, egoistic will, or selfish thought. We can only obey the Lord and let Him be the head. The Lord alone is in that position; nobody else can be. I cannot be head, neither can anyone else in the church be, for the body has only one head and is in subjection to that head, which is Christ. We all must therefore obey Him.

Unfortunately, there appears to be in the church too many heads, too many human leaders, too many men's ways and regulations. Too often man aspires to be the authority. While Christ is head in heaven, man wants to be head on earth. When the thought of the earthly head happens to agree with that of the heavenly one, we obey Christ. But when the earthly head disagrees with the heavenly one, we disobey Christ. How wrong is this entire system!

Have you ever said to the Lord: "O Lord, You are my head. I have no right to decide anything, nor have I authority to make any choice of my own. May You deliver me from trying to be head as well as deliver me from other people who set themselves up as head." Each one of us needs to learn how to accept the command of God: Christ is head, and therefore no one can follow his own will. To be subdued by the Lord and then to capitulate to Him should be a basic experience of every Christian.

We learn from Acts 2 that when Peter proclaimed the gospel he said this: "God hath made him both Lord and Christ, this Jesus whom ye crucified" (v.36). He opened his mouth and declared that Christ is Lord. Christ is not only Savior, He is firstly Lord: we need Him to be Lord to us. And because we have sinned, He must also be our Savior.

Take a look at the experience of Paul at his conversion. While he was on the way to Damascus the Lord shone around him. And then he asked: "Who art thou, Lord?"(Acts 9.5) Paul first saw Jesus as Lord before he believed on Him as Savior. Oh how we all must come to the place where we can honestly say: "O Lord, I am finished. Henceforth, it is You who directs me, because You are the Lord."

Three

Let us realize that we all must hold fast the head. To do this means to acknowledge that Christ alone is head. It means absolute obedience to His authority. "May grow up in all things into him, who is the head, even Christ; from whom all the body fitly framed and knit together through that which every joint supplieth, according to the working in due measure of each several part, maketh the increase of the body unto the building up of itself in love" (Eph. 4.15,16). From this passage we learn that the members of the body of

Christ are fitly framed and knit together because all hold fast the head and live out the life of the body. This does not suggest that God wants you to pay attention only to the one who sits next to you, but that He preeminently wants you to have a proper relationship with the Lord. If you maintain such a relationship with the head you will have a good relationship with other body members. All matters between you and your brothers and sisters may be easily solved if you can submit yourself to the head. If you have no controversy with the Lord you will have no problem with any brother or sister.

Whether or not you can successfully live out the life of the body rests on your relationship with the head. Let us see that we did not become Christians because we found other Christians agreeable, nor are we successful as believers because we have mastered some kind of Christian technique. We became Christians because we know Christ. And the way we continue to live successfully as Christians is the way we were born as Christians. We were so born by having a relationship with the head, and we continue as Christians by maintaining a proper relationship with the head—who is Christ the Lord.

This is not to insinuate that Christians do not need to have fellowship with one another; no, it simply affirms that the fellowship among believers is based on their relationship to Christ. We need to fellowship with one another because the Christ who dwells in me and the Christ who dwells in you are inseparable. The Christ who indwells me is not a fragmentary, but a whole, Christ. Christ in you and Christ in me—this is the Christ that is the basis of our fellowship. Aside from Him we have nothing with which to fellowship. Even though the education we each receive and the environment and natural talent we individually have are all different, there is still one thing common to all of us, which is the indwelling Christ. Since the Christ in us is the same, we can fellowship with one another. Not because a certain person has ability or good temper or is gentle or considerate do you have fellowship with that one. Not at all. If your fellowship is based on people, you are not holding fast the head—but on the contrary, your fellowship will be according to the kind of communication which Absalom had with the people of Israel. Such fellowship separated the people from David (see 2 Sam. 15.1–17). And similar conduct today would not constitute a holding fast the head.

The fellowship between Christians ought to be that which is related to Christ. We have no basis for fellowship outside of the head. Our fellowship is both normal and profitable if all of us hold fast the head Otherwise, fellowship will be marred. How far will you go as a Christian? Will you follow the Lord to the end? If someone draws back and falls away, will not your fellowship with him be affected? All of us must follow the Lord the entire way in order to maintain full fellowship, which only the mutual holding fast of the head can accomplish.

Four

What are the conditions for holding fast the head?

On the one hand we must let the cross deal deeply with the flesh and its natural life and on the other hand we need to learn to walk according to the Spirit. Thus shall we enjoy a wholesome body fellowship. Without the dealing of the natural life by the cross we cannot live out the body life.

The book of Revelation reveals a company of people who follow the Lamb wheresoever He goes (see 14.1–5). Can we say we follow the Lamb anywhere He goes? Let us never forget that the cross is the instrument of fellowship. It deals with our flesh, it breaks down our self-life so that we may follow the Lamb wherever He leads. If we have no hindrance before the Lord, we will present no obstruction to the church. If our relationship with the head is proper, our relationship with the body will also be proper. For let us clearly understand that every member has a direct relationship with the head. In the physical body, for example, if the left hand should be hurt, it will be the head which orders the right hand to help. The right hand makes no direct move by itself. So is it with the body of Christ. The inter-relatedness of its members comes in every instance through the head. When one member goes to help a brother, if he holds fast the head it is for the Lord's sake and not for the sake of mere human friendship. By holding fast the head we will be spared from maintaining a direct relationship with anyone, and thus we will not harbor any special affinity towards a few. To do otherwise will bring in division or party spirit.

Now God does not permit division or party in the church. What is party? A party is formed when a few

Christians establish direct intercourse among themselves through the technique of bypassing the head. They maintain a special affinity towards each other which does not originate with the head. This is party. Yet what is even worse than a party is a sect. Some people are so close and so naturally attracted to one another that they form a sectarian group. But if brethren will hold fast the head their hearts will be as large as that of the head. Brethren should indeed love one another; yet this mutual love has a foundation which belongs to the entire body of Christ. Loving one another must encompass all members in the body. That which falls short of the boundary of the body is not permitted by God. Only by holding fast the head can Christians love one another without falling into parties and sects.

4 | The Service of the Member

For even as we have many members in one body, and all the members have not the same office [function]: so we, who are many, are one body in Christ, and severally members one of another. (Rom. 12.4, 5)

One

How many of us who are Christians know that we are not only believers but also members of the body of Christ? We ought to understand that in the Adamic life there is not just the sinful or the natural which needs to be dealt with, the individualistic temper must also be dealt with. What do we mean by the individualistic character in the Adamic life? It is that attitude of life which insists on maintaining my independent existence, my independent living, or my individual action as though I were the only one living in the world. This kind of life hinders us from entering into the reality of the body of Christ. We should know that the antithesis of the body is the individual. For us to enter into the reality of the body, we must be delivered from individualism.

The body of Christ is not just a teaching. The body of Christ needs to be entered into experientially. Whoever has not entered in does not know what is within. He who is saved can easily detect whoever is saved or not; in like manner, the one who has already entered into the reality of the body of Christ may also discern quickly whether others have entered into the reality of it or not. When you are saved you have not only heard the doctrine of salvation but also seen that Christ is the living life. In salvation you enter a new realm. And after being in this new realm you are able to discern clearly the situation of the unsaved in retrospect. Similarly, those who truly live in the body of Christ may vividly perceive the conditions of all who have not lived in the body. People may understand the book of Romans and not be saved; likewise, men may appreciate the letter of Ephesians and not know the body of Christ. When you forsake sin and enter into Christ, you are saved. But you need to be delivered from being individualistic in order to enter experientially into the body of Christ.

God permits us to be individuals, but He does not allow us to be individualistic. Before we enter experientially into the body of Christ we are full of individualism. Even our spiritual pursuit is inspired by this trait. Why seek for holiness? That I myself may be holy. Why desire for power? That I personally may have power. Why look for fruits of labor? That I individually may have fruits. Why wish for the kingdom? That I myself may possess the kingdom. Everything is bound up with "I". This is not the body; this is individualism.

Just as Peter at Pentecost had saved in one day three thousand people, so I dream of saving three thousand in one day that I too may produce many fruits. Yet we need to recall that the eleven other apostles stood up with Peter. Did the other apostles ever jealously complain, saying that if Peter could save many people, they too should be able to do the same? Or did Peter ever build up in his mind a high tower of boasting, saying that he could save people whom others could not? We know that no such thing ever happened. For God does not look for an individual vessel but is out to get a corporate one. If you truly see the body of Christ you will neither be jealous nor proud. Whether the work is done by you or by me or by others makes no difference. All of this is a body matter, nothing is purely individual.

We therefore need to see ourselves not only as believers but even more so as members. I am a member; hence I am not the whole—not even the half—but only a small part of Christ's body. It is unquestionably a tremendous deliverance to see the body and to recognize oneself as only a member. Formerly many things were centered on our individual selves. Whether it was work or living, all was highly individualistic. One day when we discerned the body we were naturally delivered from individualism. In salvation we first see Christ and then we are saved. By the same token, we first see the body and then quite naturally we are de-

livered from individualism and become members of
the body in reality. Not in the sense that we outwardly
say we will act according to the principle of the body
when we are faced with a situation, but in the sense of
acting according to the principle of the body because
we have received the revelation and have entered experientially into the body of Christ. With the natural
life being dealt with, we spontaneously perceive that
we are members.

How do I live as a member of the body of Christ?
The body must be taken as the unit and boundary of
all my works and living. In the physical realm, when
my hand works, it is not my hand but my body which
works; when my feet walk, it is not my feet but my
body which walks. A physical member never does anything for its own self; whatever it does is for the sake
of the body. So too is this true in the spiritual realm.
All the actions of a member of the body of Christ are
governed by the body of Christ, not by the individual
member himself. Whether God puts me in first or in
last place, it is equally acceptable with me. For only
the one who does not see, know, and experience the
body of Christ will be proud or jealous.

We must realize the relationship which exists between the member and the body. A member cannot be
a substitute for the entire body, yet it can affect the
whole body. Personal defeat and personal unholiness
will influence it. Secret failure of an individual may
not be known by men, but the devil knows it. Hidden
defeat of a single person may not be perceived by others, yet the evil spirits know it. The defeat of one
member touches the whole church. For this reason, we

must seek after a life of love: it is for the entire body. We must pursue after a holy life: for this also is for the body's sake. We must desire spiritual progress: but it too is for the sake of the body.

Let us seriously ask ourselves: Am I an independent individualist? Or am I a member of the body? Am I just a believer? Or am I also a member? You are without doubt a Christian, but if you cannot be with other people for five minutes without having some trouble or finding yourself incompatible with others, how can you demonstrate that you live as a member? The Lord will not be satisfied with such kind of living. May God give us light that we may clearly perceive the body of Christ. And having perceived it, we will naturally be delivered from individualism and will spontaneously live as members.

Two

Each member has his part in serving the body of Christ. Everyone who belongs to the Lord has his portion. He has Christ within, and what he has in Christ has a characteristic of its own. It is this characteristic which becomes the distinctive feature of that one's service. To serve the church is to serve with what one obtains in Christ.

The portion of service which we have in the body of Christ is based on our knowledge of Him. Yet this is not a common knowledge, because a common knowledge of Christ is inadequate. Only a specific knowledge of Him will constitute a specific ministry in serving the body of Christ. Hence specific service is based on specific knowledge of the Lord. Having learned what others have not learned, you receive from the Lord a specific lesson, and with this specific knowledge of Him you may serve. In the human body, for example, the eyes can see, the ears can hear, and the nose can smell. They all have their own functions, and thus each has its own portion. Similarly with the members of the body of Christ. Not every member can see or hear or smell; but each member has his own special ability. This, then, is that member's ministry.

What is your specific ministry? That which you learn especially from the Lord, that which you specifically receive from Him. Only specific ministry can serve the church and cause the latter to increase. Only what comes from above is able to make for the increase of the body. Whatever you have learned before the Lord is what you may transmit of the life of the head to the body and what you may supply to the church which she does not already have. Hence each member needs to seek earnestly from the Lord what the church has never possessed so as to transmit this to the body of Christ. Today the Lord is looking for those people in whom life is given and by whom the work of the increase of the life of the body might be done. They are used to supply life to the church which she has never known before, to increase the measure of the stature of the Lord, and to be the channel of the life to the body. From them the life which they receive from the Lord flows into the church, thus causing the increase of the stature of the body of Christ.

To serve the body of Christ means to supply to it

the life which a member receives from the head; that is to say, he supplies the life of the head to the church. When the eyes of a seeing member see, the entire body is able to see. In other words, that member of the body of Christ who has insight into spiritual things becomes the eyes of the body so as to supply seeing to the body. Hands cannot by the sense of touch discern the odor of a thing; but the nose can; it serves the body with its ability to smell. And thus smelling becomes the specific ministry of the nose to the body. Ears, too, serve the body, but with hearing. So hearing is the specific ministry of that member of the body of Christ who can serve as the body's ears. And such can be called the service of the member. And the result of the operation of each such service will be to increase the strength of the body, causing the latter to gain more of Christ. Hence the service or ministry of the member is to serve the church with Christ, thus imparting Christ to others.

The service to the body of Christ is based on knowledge of Christ; and this knowledge comes from life experience, not from doctrine. Man often substitutes life with doctrine or teaching. This is a big mistake, since doctrine is of no avail in itself. People may hear a teaching till they can recite it or even speak on it, yet their understanding is not opened because they do not really see. People are not helped simply because they know teaching. Knowing the teaching at most only adds more thoughts to the mind. God wants to demonstrate a doctrine with life. He therefore first gives life and then the doctrine. This is true from the Old Testament to the New. For instance, God obtained the man Abraham to be the father of faith. Everyone who beholds the life of Abraham can see the doctrine of faith. Or as another example, Abel realized that without the blood no one could approach God. And hence Abel's life represents the teaching of being justified by the blood of Christ (see Rom. 5.9).

In the New Testament, we find the same thing. Please note that the Gospels precede the Epistles. The Gospels first relate what Christ has done, and only then do the later Epistles *explain* what actually has transpired. First the experience of Christ, then the doctrine of Christ. First the life of Christ, then the teaching of Christ.

First life, then doctrine. First a problem, then the solution. First an experience, then the teaching. Martin Luther went through much suffering and hardship, yet he did not obtain justification. Not until one day God showed him that justification is by faith. Only by faith was he finally justified; and thereafter he presented the teaching of justification by faith. First the life, then the applicable doctrine.

Let us not spend too much time in examining, analyzing, and researching a doctrine. All these are like reeds which will not support you when encountering real life difficulties. It is God who carries you through. First experience, then the doctrine.

If a person does not have a special experiential knowledge of Christ, that person does not have a ministry. It is through receiving in life something particular from Him that a ministry is formed. The characteristic of a member is the ministry or service of that member. The hand, for instance, has its particular characteristic, hence the latter becomes its ministry to the body. All sufferings, all disciplines, and all trials are used by God to incorporate His word in us that we may have something with which to supply the church. Apart from Christ, aside from life, there is nothing of service to the body of Christ. Christ is life: it is with Him that we supply the church for its building up. The one who has no life brings death to a meeting even if that one only says an amen in a prayer meeting. But the one who has life is able to supply life to the prayer meeting even if that one merely says an amen. Sitting with a person with life will cause people to sense the life in him. The measure of one's knowledge of Christ is the measure with which a member can supply the church with life.

Today God is seeking for people in whom He can deposit an abundant portion of the life of Christ so that they may supply others. Life needs a channel. And God wants man to be that channel of life. He will use man to transmit life to the body of Christ. If life stops in you or me, we will not be able to supply life to others and the church will suffer loss. For instead of supplying life we will spread death in the church. There is never a personal defeat which does not adversely affect the church. As a consequence, in the body of Christ, when one member suffers all the members suffer with that member. Even if a member is defeated in his room, such as in the matter of neglecting prayer, the body will surely suffer. Every member may influence others. Hence let us not live to ourselves. Let us hold fast the head and seek fellowship.

Before we make certain decisions let us have fellowship. All is in, through, and for the body—not in,
through, or for the individual. May God cause us to
see the body. May He also use our ministry to serve
the church according to our real knowledge of Christ.

5 | The Function and Harmony of the Members

For even as we have many members in one body, and all the members have not the same office [function]: so we, who are many, are one body in Christ, and severally members one of another.(Rom. 12.4,5).

For the perfecting of the saints, unto the work of ministering, unto the building up of the body of Christ: till we all attain unto the unity of the faith, and of the knowledge of the Son of God, unto a fullgrown man, unto the measure of the stature of the fulness of Christ. (Eph. 4.12,13)

But speaking truth in love, may grow up in all things into him, who is the head, even Christ; from whom all the body fitly framed and knit together through that which every joint supplieth, according to the working in due measure of each several part, maketh the increase of the body unto the building up of itself in love. (Eph. 4. 15,16)

The Function of the Members

To the one who lives for the Lord and is delivered
from self, the most important part of his external life
is that he might manifest his function in the church.
Most certain is it that each member in the body of
Christ has his place. If you as a member fail to express your function, it only proves that outwardly you
have not lived for the Lord nor inwardly have you
been delivered from yourself. Had you truly been delivered from your own self, you would have spontaneously exhibited your particular office in the church.
You as a brother or you as a sister each have a measure or portion of a particular function in the church.
However much you may feel you have been delivered
from yourself and are living for the Lord, your feeling
is not only inaccurate but also a deception if you cannot manifest your function as a member in the church.
If in fact you *have* been delivered from yourself and
truly are living for the Lord, one thing in your life will
be most certain, which is, that you will automatically
manifest in the body that portion of a special function
or office which you have as a brother or a sister.

Never for a moment think that because the grace
you have received is so insignificant you therefore
have no place in the church. As long as you are a
member, you have a definite function. There is no one
having the life of God who is not a member of the
body of Christ, and no member is so small as to have
no function of his own. The less than the least of the
members still has his function in the body, and that
particular function cannot be replaced by any other

member. No matter how tiny is that function, no one else can substitute it. Not even the greatest function in the body can stand in for the smallest one: none can take the place of the other: you cannot be a substitute for me, nor can I be a substitute for you. Oh, if we could see this we would leap for joy!

In this connection, please notice that the Gospels of the New Testament are written by four different persons. When you read the Gospel according to Matthew, you see one aspect of Christ; in reading the Gospel according to Mark, you discern another side of Christ; in reading the Gospel according to Luke, still another aspect of the holiness of Christ is in view; and reading the Gospel according to John, yet another facet of the glory of Christ is seen. Moreover, if you read Peter's epistles you behold the splendor of Christ; in reading Paul's epistles, there is given still another presentation of Christ; and in perusing the epistles of John, you must confess that his description of the glorious beauty of Christ excels anything that has ever been written. From all this it must be concluded that our Lord is so great that it requires believers of all ages and from all nations to express Him. Do please understand that the outflow of life is the expression of Christ; and the body of Christ is where this life is manifested in all of its varied beauty and glory through the body's members.

Life, we must see, is a unit whole, but it is expressed by means of various offices or functions as it is manifested through different members. When this life of Christ flows to the ears, there is hearing; when it flows to the eyes, there is seeing; when it flows to the feet, there is walking; when it flows to the mouth, there is speaking; and when it flows to the teeth, there is chewing. This life is indeed one, yet the functions are many; and though of many functions, they are still from the one life. That which flows into you and into me is the same life of Christ, but the functions operative in you and in me are different.

Frequently, what one brother can do, no one else can do it in quite the same way. With respect to a certain matter in the church, you must seek out a certain brother; whereas with respect to another matter, you must seek out a particular sister. But just you change the brother or the sister and the result will be that that matter will not be done. As a particular member in the body, you have your specific office. And the office which is operative in you as the life of Christ flows into you is something which no other person can be a substitute for. Regardless of how small you as a member are, you have your place.

Brethren may test themselves in this matter quite simply: If today in a local assembly you have yet to manifest your function—and not because of the smallness of your function but because your presence or absence in the church seems rather optional—then this is sufficient proof that neither outwardly do you live for the Lord nor inwardly is your life delivered from self. This is a very concrete test.

Satan's Work of Disintegration

We ought to know that in order to spread His

gospel, do His work, and fulfill His will on earth, the Lord must use His body. Neither His will nor His way can be realized through one person, since the Lord does not work through one man but through the church. The vessel God will use is the church, not an individual. The life and power of Christ find their richest manifestation through the body of Christ. For this reason, Satan takes great pains to try to effect the "disintegration" of the body of Christ. This becomes his number one task. If we take note of this, we will readily realize how severe is this Satanic work of "disintegration": suspicion arises among brothers and sisters, misunderstanding is easily created. This is Satan doing his disintegrating work. One of us is blaming a brother, and the latter is murmuring against a sister. Yet if the cause is investigated, there is nothing serious about it at all. This too is Satan performing his work of tearing down the body. Satan induces God's children to divide; he causes them to disintegrate as a body. The work of God is to make us one body, but the work of Satan is to cause us to be torn asunder. Satan uses our corrupted flesh, our stubborn self, and the world which we covet to carry out his work of destruction. Hence actually the serious problem here does not lie in our not having the flesh dealt with, nor in our not laying down ourselves, neither in our living according to the world—but it rests upon the fact that it is Satan who will use these weaknesses of ours to do the work of tearing and dividing. If these elements are permitted to remain in our lives, we clearly make room for Satan to work his work of disintegration.

What, in truth, is our understanding of oneness?
Quite simply, oneness is God himself. Why is this so?
Because when all of us set aside the things outside of
God and begin to live in Him, then God who is in us
becomes the oneness. Oneness is when God has His
absolute place in us. Oneness is when He alone is in
all, when He fills all. When the children of God are
filled with God, they harmonize with one another. As
a matter of fact, Satan, in his attempt to effect the
disintegration of us as a body, does not need to stir up
opinions and strife among us so long as he is able to
plant some impurity in us or something else which
takes the place of God. As an illustration of this, have
you ever noticed how people mix concrete? If there is
some clay blended with the sand, the cement will not
firmly congeal. Now for Satan to destroy our oneness
in the body, he needs to do nothing but spread a little
mud—that which is incompatible with the life of God
in us—and we as a body shall disintegrate. Neither
opinions nor strifes are necessary, merely the spread-
ing of a little mud in us is enough. We continue to
break bread and drink the cup, but we may be divided
nonetheless.

The body of Christ is basically not a doctrine, neither is it a kind of arrangement, but it essentially is
life. What is the church? The church is not just a doctrine according to the Scriptures; neither is it just a
method according to the Scriptures; but basically it is
a life, even the manifestation of the life of Christ.
Oneness is not grounded in anything else but in life.
Satan needs only to mix some impurities into us and

into others secretly; so that though among us all there is not the slightest clamor of opinions or the slightest indication of strife, nevertheless, unknowingly the body is already undergoing disintegration. May the Lord have mercy on us by the filtering out of all impurities from us. O Lord, by the cross and the Holy Spirit, do filter us out!

How we all need to inquire as to what place does our own inclination and desires have in us: What place does our own goal have in us? What place does our own work have in us? Or do we let the life of Christ occupy the absolute position in us? Oh how we all need to return to God! We do not need outward revival. We have but one need, which is, to turn inwardly to God and let Him cleanse us and purify us with the cross and the Holy Spirit. By the filtering of the cross and the Holy Spirit, we hope and pray we may be cleansed from all the impurities which Satan has mixed into us. May the Lord have mercy upon us so that we may not put our confidence in ourselves, for even that sense in us of being right may be used by Satan to work the work of disintegration. We should learn to come to God for enlightening, we should learn to go among brothers and sisters for correction. We must be willing to pay any cost and accept the dealing of the cross in order that we may truly manifest our functions as members in the church.

Do we not continually say we love the Lord? Do we not say we have consecrated ourselves to Him? Then we must not preserve ourselves, neither should we be afraid of paying any cost; but we should allow the Lord to cleanse us from all the impurities which are incompatible so that the life of Christ may be expressed through us and that we may manifest in our life our various functions as body members as well as live out the testimony of the body of Christ.

6 | Obeying the Law of the Body of Christ

They therefore that were scattered abroad went about preaching the word. And Philip went down to the city of Samaria, and proclaimed unto them the Christ. And the multitudes gave heed with one accord unto the things that were spoken by Philip, when they heard, and saw the signs which he did. For from many of these that had unclean spirits, they came out, crying with a loud voice: and many that were palsied, and that were lame, were healed. And there was much joy in that city. (Acts 8.4–8)

But when they believed Philip preaching good tidings concerning the kingdom of God and the name of Jesus Christ, they were baptized, both men and women. (Acts 8.12)

Now when the apostles that were at Jerusalem heard that Samaria had received the word of God, they sent unto them Peter and John: who, when they were come down, prayed for them, that they might receive the Holy Spirit: for as yet it was fallen upon none of them: only they had been baptized into the name of the Lord Jesus.

Then laid they their hands on them, and they received the Holy Spirit. (Acts 8.14–17)

Lay hands hastily on no man, neither be partaker of other men's sins: keep thyself pure. (1 Tim. 5.22)

Neglect not the gift that is in thee, which was given thee by prophecy, with the laying on of the hands of the presbytery. (1 Tim. 4.14)

For which cause I put thee in remembrance that thou stir up the gift of God, which is in thee through the laying on of my hands. (2 Tim. 1.6)

Is any among you sick? let him call for the elders of the church; and let them pray over him, anointing him with oil in the name of the Lord: and the prayer of faith shall save him that is sick, and the Lord shall raise him up; and if he have committed sins, it shall be forgiven him. Confess therefore your sins one to another, and pray one for another, that ye may be healed. The supplication of a righteous man availeth much in its working. (James 5.14–16)

And as he journeyed, it came to pass that he drew nigh unto Damascus: and suddenly there shone round about him a light out of heaven: and he fell upon the earth, and heard a voice saying unto him, Saul, Saul, why persecutest thou me? And he said, Who art thou, Lord? And he said, I am Jesus whom thou persecutest: but rise, and enter into the city, and it shall be told thee what thou must do. . . .But the Lord said unto him [Ananias], Go thy way: for he is a chosen vessel unto me, to bear my name before the Gentiles and kings, and the children of Israel: for I will show him how many things he must suffer for my name's sake. And Ananias departed, and entered into the house; and laying his hands on him said, Brother Saul, the Lord, even Jesus, who appeared unto thee in the way which thou camest, hath sent me, that thou mayest receive thy sight, and be filled with the Holy Spirit. (Acts 9.3–17)

And if thy brother sin against thee, go, show him his fault between thee and him alone: if he hear thee, thou hast gained thy brother. But if he hear thee not, take with thee one or two more, that at the mouth of two witnesses or three every word may be established. And if he refuse to hear them, tell it unto the church: and if he refuse to hear the church also, let him be unto thee as the Gentile and the publican. (Matt. 18.15–17)

If we wish to live the life of the body of Christ, we must first receive the revelation of the body of Christ. Without such revelation we will never cease to move individualistically. Some people deem the seeing of the body of Christ as not a surprising thing at all, but let us realize that we cannot speak empty words. For if anyone has really apprehended the body of Christ he must readily acknowledge that it has its own inherent law according to which he must live continually. Anyone who has seen Christ will not trust in his good deeds for salvation. By the same token, a person who says he has seen the body of Christ and yet continually acts independently by not holding fast the head has never received the revelation of the body. For had he truly received such revelation, he would be bound to change. He would seek out fellowship and would learn submission.

The Authority of Life

No member has any authority, for authority rests only in the head. It is a serious mistake for a member to claim he has such authority in himself. A member does not possess direct authority; he has only the authority delegated to him by the head. And this authority is not something positional, it is wholly of life. Such authority does not come through "appointment" but by "being": If a member is not an eye, the body has no way to appoint him as its eye. If he is not a hand, the body cannot make him a hand through appointment. He has the authority of holding or of seeing only because he can hold or see. And as he functions along that line, people receive help.

It is a serious blunder if, in a church, authority becomes a matter of position and not of life—if a person is appointed because of his social position and not because of his spirituality. The word of God plainly shows us that authority is in life, not in position or background. Authority in a person is established in living, not in ordination. In his personal and corporate life he has experienced dealings in practical matters and has learned what other people have yet to learn. In the body of Christ, all authorities are out of life.

Although in a local assembly God has His appointment, even so, such appointment is not according to position, but according to life. When life and appointment agree, you must submit; otherwise, life will cease and you will be dislocated from the body—thus signifying that you do not hold fast the head. If something is wrong between you and another member, you cannot say you have a normal relationship with the head. If you have wronged another member of the body, you subsequently may not forget any teaching and you may even continue to carry on a work of ministry as usual, but you lose the word of life. Some brethren may have believed in the Lord for three years now. Yet how much real progress have they made? What is most pitiful is that though their courtesy and knowledge may have appeared to have increased, the life of the body of Christ in them has not increased.

Hence in the church we need to learn how to submit to one another. If members do not mutually submit, the life mentioned in Romans 8 will not be able to be manifested. On the contrary, brethren will feel as though air were leaking out of them—they can hardly go on. But to those who have discerned the body of Christ, they consider submission to be a most joyful thing.

In Acts 8 we have a case which illustrates the law of the body. When the church at Jerusalem suffered its first great persecution, all the brethren with the exception of the apostles were scattered abroad. Those who were scattered went about preaching the word of God. Now Philip was not an apostle, for his ministry in Jerusalem lay in serving the tables. Yet there was much life in him. And he went down to the city of Samaria and proclaimed Christ to the people there. Signs were performed by him, and unclean spirits were cast out from many of them, and many who were palsied and lame were healed. The entire city was filled with the sound of the gospel. And the Bible account notes that "there was much joy in the city"(v.8)

—thus indicating that there were multitudes who believed.

Being so mightily used by the Lord, Philip, had he wished to, could have proudly declared that though in Jerusalem it was Peter who saved souls, in Samaria the one who saved souls was Philip himself. He could have regarded himself as a great man in history. Yet after Philip had preached the gospel in Samaria, the experience of those who were saved turned out to be different from the experience of those who had been saved in Jerusalem—because in Samaria the Holy Spirit had not fallen on any of them. These Samaritans had truly believed and they had been baptized in the name of the Lord Jesus, but the Holy Spirit had not fallen on any of them. Now when the apostles in Jerusalem heard about this, they sent Peter and John to Samaria. And after their arrival, they prayed for the new converts that they might receive the Holy Spirit. The apostles laid their hands on them, and thus they received the Holy Spirit.

What is the meaning of the incident of the laying on of hands? The book of Leviticus tells us that during the offering of a sacrifice hands of the one doing the offering were laid on the head of the animal sacrifice. What does this laying hands on the sacrifice represent? Only the bullocks which had hands laid on them could be offered up; the rest of the bullocks in the world could not be offered. Why? Simply this, that the laying of hands on the bullock joins the one who lays hands and the bullock into one. The bullock becomes the offerer. In offering up the bullock, the offerer actually offers up himself. As the bullock is accepted, so too is he accepted. And hence, the basic meaning of the laying on of hands is union.

The New Testament also mentions the laying on of hands a number of times. One place is found in 1 Timothy: "Lay hands hastily on no man, neither be partaker of other men's sins: keep thyself pure" (5.22). Since the laying on of hands is a being joined together with other people, it will make a person partaker of other men's sins if he is not careful in doing so. Laying on of hands means union, which in turn means fellowship. In the Old Testament times, at the commissioning of kings and priests, hands were laid on their heads as well as oil was poured on their heads. Consequently, the laying on of hands means, firstly, the bringing of men under the anointing of the head and, secondly, the bringing of them into the fellowship of the body.

Today, in the church, the apostles are the representative members of the body of Christ. They also represent the authority of Christ. As the apostles laid hands on the believers in Samaria they recognized the latter as now being in the body. As soon as these believers entered the body, the Holy Spirit descended upon them. Suppose the saved in Samaria had received the Holy Spirit before the arrival of the apostles; then Philip might have been led to think that if the apostles knew how to work in Jerusalem, he also would know how to work in Samaria—with the consequence being that the saved in Samaria would have had no connection with the saved in Jerusalem. And thus, to say that Jerusalem has Peter and Samaria has Philip would have been to destroy the prin-

ciple of the body. For if such had been the case, the
work which God had done in Jerusalem and the work
which He had done in Samaria would have been two
separate works, not one undifferentiated work in two
places. For this reason, this incident in Samaria was
important in that it caused the believers in Samaria to
see that unless they had submitted to the one body of
Christ there would have been no anointing. They had
to wait until the apostles had come from Jerusalem
and had laid their hands on them. For only then did
the Holy Spirit fall upon them.

How we need to see that the Holy Spirit is the Spirit of the one body, not the Spirit of an individual. And
if so, then it is basically wrong to seek the Holy Spirit
for the sake of one's own self. Why is it that some
people are deceived? Why, for example, are some believers the recipients of evil spirits? It is because of
their individualism—because of their not apprehend-
ing the body. The kind of vessel which the Lord looks
for today is a corporate one, not an individual one. Individual work and individual fruit can never fully sat-
isfy the Lord's heart, neither will they ever attain to
God's ultimate aim. The principle of the laying on of
hands must be in every work. In such laying on of
hands is the recognition of union. In the laying on of
hands is the acknowledgment of fellowship. In the laying on of hands is the confession of one body.

"Wherefore leaving the doctrine of the first principles of Christ, let us press on unto perfection; not laying again a foundation of repentance from dead
works, and of faith toward God, of the teaching of
baptisms, and of laying on of hands, and of resurrec-

tion of the dead, and of eternal judgment" (Heb. 6.1,2). Here we find six matters which constitute the doctrine of the first principles of Christ, and these six can be divided into three groups of two each: namely, that the first group includes two actions; the second, two external testimonies; and the third, two teachings concerning the future. Repentance from dead works and faith towards God are two actions; baptism and the laying on of hands represent two external testimonies; and the resurrection of the dead and eternal judgment form two teachings with respect to the future. It is interesting that we today do not neglect five of these six, but the one concerning the laying on of hands we do overlook. Even though the Bible does not have an explicit command about the laying on of hands, we cannot deny the fact that people who were saved during the apostolic days received the laying on of hands immediately after they were baptized. Baptism is unto Christ, the laying on of hands is unto the body. In the laying on of hands, a believer testifies as to his relationship with the body as well as to his relationship with Christ. It speaks of the fact that he is to submit to the authority of the head and not to act independently, that he is to deny individualism in work as well as in living.

"Whether one member suffereth," says Paul, "all the members suffer with it; or one member is honored, all the members rejoice with it" (1 Cor. 12.26). With the laying on of hands, a believer is giving testimony to his having been delivered from individualism and his having become a member of the body of Christ. When a person receives the laying on of hands, he does so for the sake of desiring to stand in his proper place in the body.

Imparting Gift through the Laying On of Hands

"I put thee in remembrance," said Paul to Timothy, "that thou stir up the gift of God, which is in thee through the laying on of my hands" (2 Tim. 1.6). What is meant here is that the gift which young Timothy received when he had experienced the laying on of hands must be stirred up and revived. Moreover, elsewhere Paul said this to Timothy: "Neglect not the gift that is in thee, which was given thee by prophecy, with the laying on of hands of the presbytery" (1 Tim. 4.14). In the instance referred to here, the apostle plus the eldership had imparted a gift to Timothy by prophecy. The one who gives a gift is of course the divine Anointing. When Paul and the elders laid hands on Timothy and prayed, God gave to one of them a prophetic prayer which predicted what kind of person Timothy would be in the future. And this prayer regulated the giving of the gift. When one who has had deep experience with the Lord lays his hands on people, the content of his prayer shall become the characteristic of the person who receives the laying on of hands. For here the authority of the head is transmitted through a representative member, and thus a proper gift is granted to the one who receives the laying on of hands.

All who have had the laying on of hands should see that thereafter they have become a part of the body: thereafter they will not seek spirituality for their personal profit but for the good of the body. From now on, whether the Lord uses them or uses somebody else makes no difference. They will not be jealous when another member is being used. Oh how many works are done on an individual basis, oh how much seeking is for personal spiritual profit! May God deliver us from all these even as He has delivered us from sin.

Pray with Anointing

"Is any among you sick? let him call for the elders of the church; and let them pray over him, anointing him with oil in the name of the Lord" (James 5.14). This verse should be read together with a passage in 1 Corinthians 11: "He that eateth and drinketh, eateth and drinketh judgment unto himself, if he discern not the body. For this cause many among you are weak and sickly, and not a few sleep" (vv.29,30). There are many reasons for sickness: some are due to the violation of natural physiological laws, but some are due to the violation of the law of the body of Christ. If a Christian does not discern the body and does not follow the law of the body, he will be subject to weakness and sickness. For sickness of this kind, he must ask the elders to come. These elders are appointed by God in the local assembly. They are representative members. They represent the body of Christ in the locality. They will come and anoint the sick with oil.

". . . the precious oil upon the head, that ran down upon the beard, even Aaron's beard; that came down upon the skirt of his garments" (Ps. 133.2). In the olden days of the priesthood the oil was poured on

Aaron the high priest's head and it then flowed from his head to the skirt of his garments. The Oil of God is upon the head of Christ, for the Holy Spirit is given to the Son. And thus Christians receive the anointing under the headship of Christ their High Priest. Why must this sick person ask the elders to come and anoint him with oil? When a person is sick, you may readily recognize what his sickness is by knowing the medicine which the doctor has prescribed or given him. Here in James the apostle has told us what God has prescribed for the one who is sick. He is to ask the elders to come and anoint him with oil. Anointing with oil is what is prescribed for the person's sickness. So why then this prescription? It is simply because he has lost the anointing. Had he stood in the proper place as a member should have, he would not have lost the anointing and would not have therefore fallen sick. But because he does not discern the body, therefore he is sick. Under such a circumstance, what will the elders do? They will bring the sick one back under the head and cause him to return to the body. If the believer lives in the body, he will not lose the anointing; but if he walks out of the body, he will either be sick or become dead. Do let us understand from this that it is well if we really discern the life of the body and live therein.

The sickness mentioned in James 5 is thus a special kind of sickness. How do we know his sickness is a special one and not a general one? Because in the following verse the apostle writes this: "And the prayer of faith shall save him that is sick, and the Lord shall raise him up; and if he have committed sins, it shall be forgiven him" (v.15). What sin has he committed? Here his sin must have been the leaving of the body of Christ. Had the sin he committed been of a personal nature, all he would have needed to have done was to have trusted the precious Blood, and if necessary to have confessed it to any other people involved and had it dealt with. And he then would have been forgiven. He would not need to ask the elders to come and anoint him with oil in order to receive such forgiveness. The anointing with oil by the elders cannot get rid of sin: it is the Blood that washes sins away. Nevertheless, what is written here is that "if he have committed sins, it shall be forgiven him"; and this forgiveness comes through the prayer of the elders. Hence this sin is different from the ordinary kind. This is the sin of disharmony with the body. Such kind of sin will not be forgiven even if he himself prays to God. He needs the brethren, he needs the elders to come and pray for him. Only then will he be forgiven. He needs the help of others.

The next verse is very special: "Confess therefore your sins one to another, and pray one for another, that ye may be healed. The supplication of a righteous man availeth much in its working" (v.16). Why does it mention here to "confess therefore your sins one to another"? Simply because there is something wrong in the body of Christ and there is therefore need to confess sins one to another. The sick one must confess his sins to the elders, and vice versa. This shows us that when one member is wrong, the entire body is responsible. In the body of Christ, if one member is sick, then the elders of the entire church have their responsibility. Perhaps the elders do not show enough love or care. They need to confess this sin. The sick person, of course, must also confess his sin—the sin of being independent and of being out of touch with the body.

They must not only confess one to another, but also "pray one for another": the elders will again pray for the sick, and the sick will pray for the elders. This sufficiently shows the need for love and humility in the church. When a person falls away from the body, he is not only sick physically but also sick spiritually. For whenever he is out of touch with the body, he is out from under the anointing. How important it is for him to see the need of returning to the anointing and to the body.

The Revelation Paul Received at Repentance

Acts 9 shows us that at the time of Paul's repentance the revelation he received contained two aspects. As he traveled on the road to Damascus, a light from heaven suddenly shone on him. He fell to the ground and heard a voice saying to him: "Saul, Saul, why persecutest thou me?" The Lord is saying, "Why persecutest thou me?": He does not say, "Why persecutest thou those who believe in me?" And so Paul asked: "Who art thou, Lord?" To which the Lord answered: "I am Jesus whom thou persecutest" (vv.3–5). Here the Lord demonstrated to Paul that all who believe in Him are one with Him. Such was the first aspect of God's revelation to Paul; namely, the intimate, indivisible oneness between the head and the body. Paul was the first one in the Bible who saw the testimony of the body of Christ. No one can touch the member without at the same time touching the head. For this reason, let us never think we can sin against our brother without concomitantly sinning against Christ. Let us ever be reminded that whoever touches even the smallest member of the body touches the very head of the body. He who is hurt is the member; but he who feels it is the head.

Paul was a man greatly used by God. Yet on the road to Damascus, the Lord said to him: "Rise, and enter into the city and it shall be told thee what thou must do" (v.6). What the Lord meant by this was: I will not tell you what you are to do, but somebody else will do so. The Lord used someone else to tell Paul. This is a revelation of the body, and this second aspect of God's revelation to Paul is equally as great as the first aspect. On the first day of Paul's salvation, the Lord revealed to him the law or principle of the body. Though Paul is to be a vessel mightily used by the Lord, the Lord nevertheless uses other people to help him. Hence let us never think we do not need to depend on others as though we are to get everything directly from God alone. True, this is not meant to teach us to follow other people blindly, but it does admonish us not to entertain such a lofty attitude wherein we believe we by ourselves may receive the word of the Lord and solve all problems singlehandedly.

Note what happened to Paul: "And Saul arose from the earth; and when his eyes were opened, he saw nothing; and they led him by the hand, and brought him into Damascus. And he was three days without sight, and did neither eat nor drink" (vv.8–9). Paul had already entered the city, but for three days no one came to tell him what he should do. What if he had grown impatient? After three days, though, Ananias came. Who was this Ananias? Before this incident, we have never seen or heard of his name; and even afterwards, we shall hear no more of him. He was not a man of fame, yet the Lord apprehended him with authority and used him to help one of the greatest apostles. The understanding of a great apostle was opened to him not by himself but by a little known brother. When Ananias beheld Saul (soon to become Paul), he laid his hands on him and said: "Brother Saul, the Lord, even Jesus, who appeared unto thee in the way which thou camest, hath sent me, that thou mayest receive thy sight, and be filled with the Holy Spirit" (v.17). His laying hands on Paul and saying "Brother Saul" was for the purpose of showing to Paul the body. And for Paul to be filled with the Holy Spirit is to bring him under the anointing.

Many times the leading of the Holy Spirit in us is to bring us to receive another's leading and to accept help from others. If we do not accept another's help, we will miss out on much the Lord has for us. Some Christians decide everything by their own personal feeling. Where, then, is the body? Such believers live entirely in the individual realm; they do not see or experience the body.

Brethren ought to recall their past and take inventory as to how many actions of theirs were in the realm of the body. We each must see this: that I am a member, that I am restricted by the body, that I will receive help from other members in the church. May

God show each of us the body now. Yet just what kind of a man is he who perceives the body? He is a person who seeks for fellowship, who fears that he himself may be wrong, and who dare not work independently. Such is the person who has discerned the body.

The Judgment of the Brethren

The following words from Matthew 18 are rather marvelous: "And if thy brother sin against thee, go, show him his fault between thee and him alone: if he hear thee, thou hast gained thy brother. But if he hear thee not, take with thee one or two more, that at the mouth of two witnesses or three every word may be established" (vv.15,16). What is said here is not whether you yourself feel any wrong or not; but rather that if two or three brothers say you are wrong, you must be wrong. The emphasis is on whether anything is wrong, not whether you feel something is wrong

Suppose, for example, that a brother declares to you: "You have sinned against me in a certain matter", but that you are not aware of anything being wrong. So you go to pray. After praying, you still are not conscious of any wrong. And thus you tell your brother as follows: "Though you say I have sinned against you, I do not feel I have wronged you. I have prayed, and still I have no sense of having wronged you. I did not pray carelessly. I really prayed earnestly about it. I am not conscious of any wrong. It is not that I refuse to acknowledge a wrong; on the contrary, I am anxious to confess any sin. Nevertheless, I do not see anything wrong here." Your brother will then go and tell some other brothers. After hearing the matter, they all come to you and say you are wrong. Being a humble person, you would not at all refuse to confess a sin, yet you cannot in this instance confess, since you see no wrong. So you will go pray again, but still there is no change in your inner sentiment about the matter. Nonetheless, the Lord says that if your brothers all say you are wrong, you must be wrong whether you feel you have been wrong or not.

Another verse in Matthew 18 makes the issue even clearer. It tells us the reason why I must be wrong when I do not feel so and yet the brethren say I am wrong: "For where two or three are gathered together unto my name, there am I in the midst of them" (v.20 Darby). Some people take this verse to be a promise. This is not accurate. The Lord does not give this verse to serve as a basis for asking His presence. What this Scripture verse says is that where two or three are gathered unto the name of the Lord, there will He be in the midst of them. To be gathered together to the name of the Lord signifies the abandoning of individualism (that is, that nothing is now according to one's self) and the standing on the ground of the body of Christ. Since Christ is in all of them, there He is in the midst of them. Where two or three deny themselves and stand for Christ, the Lord will manifest himself. True harmony expresses the body. If we are found standing on the ground of the body of Christ, the Lord's authority is present. With Christ in their midst, they can represent the body. And hence, when other brothers see the fault which you yourself fail to see, you should listen to the two or three rather than to yourself. This is not meant to suggest that you blindly listen to the word of others. Only if the two or three really deny themselves and are gathered to the name of the Lord is it wise for you to accept the judgment of others rather than trust in your own judgment.

In the church there are four classes of people who represent the body: (1) the apostles; (2) the elders; (3) an individual believer specially sent by the Lord, such as in the case of Ananias being specifically sent to speak to Paul; and (4) two or three believers who deny themselves and gather themselves to the name of the Lord. These four classes of people represent the body. In the event you are wrong about something, the Lord may specially send to you a single believer to tell you wherein you are wrong. If you do not listen to a single believer, the latter will tell it to two or three others; and these two or three believers will then speak to you. If you will still not listen, you next will need the help of the elders. You cannot afford to act independently.

In many unsolved matters you need to seek out the elders and the apostles, because they are especially chosen by the Lord to represent the body. The apostles and the elders should be notified concerning any important affairs so that they may help you in unclear situations. We must not neglect the body nor those who represent it, else we shall not be able to live out the life of the church. May the Lord give us not only the revelation of the body so that we may have the testimony of the body but also grace to submit to those who represent it.

As soon as a person receives salvation he should be

brought immediately into the fellowship of the body of Christ. May the Lord enable us to obey the body as well as to obey the Lord. May He deliver us from individual, independent action and cause us to live out fully the life of the body of Christ.

7 | The Covering, Restraint, and Supply of the Body of Christ

And he put all things in subjection under his feet, and gave him to be head over all things to the church, which is his body, the fulness of him that filleth all in all. (Eph. 1.22, 23)

From whom all the body fitly framed and knit together through that which every joint supplieth, according to the working in due measure of each several part, maketh the increase of the body unto the building up of itself in love. (Eph. 4.16)

Subjecting yourselves one to another in the fear of Christ. (Eph. 5.21)

Finally, be strong in the Lord, and in the strength of his might. Put on the whole armor of God, that ye may be able to stand against the wiles of the devil. For our wrestling is not against flesh and blood, but against the principalities, against the powers, against the world-rulers of this darkness, against the spiritual hosts of wickedness in the heavenly places. Wherefore take up the whole armor of God, that ye may be able to with-

stand in the evil day, and, having done all, to stand.
Stand therefore, having girded your loins with truth, and
having put on the breastplate of righteousness, and having shod your feet with the preparation of the gospel of
peace; withal taking up the shield of faith, wherewith ye
shall be able to quench all the fiery darts of the evil one.
And take the helmet of salvation, and the sword of the
Spirit, which is the word of God: with all prayer and supplication praying at all seasons in the Spirit, and watch-
ing thereunto in all perseverance and supplication for all
the saints. (Eph. 6.10–18)

In this chapter we shall look into a few more matters related to the body of Christ. These matters are
(1) the covering of the body, (2) the restraint of the
body, and (3) the supply of the body.

The Covering of the Body

As we have seen, the church is the body of Christ
and every Christian is a member of that body. The
body of Christ not only supplies but also protects its
members. The body protection to each member is especially seen in spiritual warfare. Such protection is of
utmost importance. One reason why a child of God is
attacked by the devil is because he is too individualistic and thus he lacks the protection of the body. How
very foolish and dangerous for anyone to expose himself in the days of spiritual conflict. Because such a
person is not under the covering of the body Satan is
given opportunity to attack.

We should understand that spiritual warfare belongs to the church, not to an individual. The Epistle to the Ephesians is a letter which deals with the body of Christ. In its first chapter this letter speaks of how God has blessed us with every spiritual blessing in the heavenly places so that we may know the power of His Son's resurrection. In the same chapter it also shows us how the Lord Jesus is the head of the church and how the church is the body of Christ—the vessel which contains Christ. How exceedingly rich is the church because she is filled with Christ who fills all and in all. In the second chapter Paul tells us the origin of the body of Christ. Although the church is so rich, she should not forget her former state. She is in possession of such a rich position because of the salvation of God in redeeming her from her fallen condition. The third chapter deals with the mystery of God which reveals how both the Gentiles and the Jews are being brought together to form one new man in Christ. Chapter 4 unveils how God will build up the body of Christ and cause it to increase gradually in stature. And chapter 5 emphasizes the need for us to accept the restraint of the body since the church is the body of Christ. And finally, chapter 6 mentions the armor of the body: "Put on the whole armor of God, that ye may be able to stand" (v.11). Please notice that it is "you" plural and not "you" singular who are to put on the whole armor of God. This one special armor is for this one entire body. True, each member has his peculiar feature. But only by putting all these peculiar features together can there be the whole armor of God that then makes the body fit for spiritual warfare.

In view of this fact, let us not forget that this spiritual armor is given to the church and not to anyone individually. You as an individual cannot cope with Satan. It requires the church to deal with the enemy. What you as an individual cannot see and safeguard, other members see and guard against. Satan is not afraid of your personal prayer, but he trembles indeed when a few pray together. Some members of the body are given faith in large proportion which then can serve as a shield for your protection. Some others have the word of God in a special measure, and this can stand as the sword of the Holy Spirit. When one or several of them wield the sword—that is, when he or they use the word of God—this serves to help you. We must realize that spiritual warfare is preeminently a *joint* battle. It is not something that you are to get into singlehandedly. If you go to the fight alone, you draw the attention of Satan to yourself for his assault.

Whoever has not seen the body thinks he is competent for anything and that he himself is everything. Such a person is very easily defeated. A single tree may quite readily be severed from the soil, but a whole forest of trees cannot so easily be swept away by the wind. Satan looks for such solitary and uncovered persons to attack. He assaults the independent and the isolated. But whoever is under the covering of the body of Christ is protected, for the body has this specific function: to serve as a protective covering.

As his special target of attack Satan cannot pick on one who has the covering of the body. But the person who is not under this covering is liable to fall should he ever be attacked. This has been demonstrated many times over by the experience of numerous Christians. For example, there once was a brother who suffered ill-health. Yet this was due to the fact that he was an isolated, independent believer before the Lord. For since he did not have the covering of the body of Christ, he was attacked by Satan for his self-confidence and self-reliance. Let us realize that self-exposure is most dangerous, that self-confidence and self-reliance are extremely perilous. If *worldly* warfare needs protective covering, how much more is covering required in *spiritual* warfare! A good brother who tries to act alone creates his own snare!

Many spiritual failures and defeats can be attributed to no other reason than our being single-handed without the covering of the body. We by ourselves are each of us but one member of the body, and consequently we cannot live without the protection of other brothers and sisters. Even Moses hands needed the support of Aaron and Hur (see Ex. 17.12). If even Moses needed the support of other members, what about us?

The gates of Hades cannot prevail against the church. This very thing the Lord Jesus himself promised and declared (see Matt. 16.18). Yet our Lord has never promised God's children that they could be independent or leave the church. Spiritual warfare is not a personal affair, it is a body task. And hence, in order to obtain the needed protection, we must go to the brethren. Let us never think of ourselves as individually competent and "go it alone"—for such will only mean self-inflicted suffering.

Yet how can anyone depend on the brethren if his

natural life has not been dealt with? It is obvious that the person whose natural life remains untouched can neither trust God nor trust the brethren. No self-dependent, self-conceited person is able to walk together with the brethren. So God looks for people who know the inadequacy of themselves and who consequently seek protection among the brethren. The vessel which God needs is a whole body composed of those who recognize that they are but individual members who are in need of the help of the body. If anyone among the brothers and sisters is never joined to others and always acts according to his own will, that one is bound to fall.

Is there not even one brother or sister with whom you could consult? Is there truly no one with whom you could pray? Let me say that if ever you miss the body you lose your covering and are thereby exposed to great danger. Do not be so careless, for even in earthly war there is the need for covering. In earthly warfare, not seeking for cover when covering is needed is against every sound rule of good strategy and constitutes a dangerous flirtation with death. How very true this is in spiritual warfare as well. If ever you lose protection but do not incur any danger, rest assured that this is only because of God's special mercy and not an evidence that you are well-versed in sound spiritual strategy.

The Restraint of the Body

Since we are but members of the body of Christ we should never think of ourselves as being everything. Being individual members, we ought to accept the restraint of the body. If in the church you are a hand, you must not only be happy to be a hand but also be glad to receive the restraints which come from other members. Do not let the hand move independently. Each part of the body is under the restraint of the body; none can take individualistic liberty. Suppose, for instance, that you now need to take a trip. Even if some member in your physical body is too lazy to move, it must nonetheless go with your body. It is inconceivable that your body could go away and leave that particular member at home. In just such a manner are we to be the members of the body of Christ. We must be joined in one with other brothers and sisters.

The work of the cross, besides bringing us *into* the body, has its sphere of operation *within* the body as well. If we are merely members to each other as those in a *congregation* are, we may not need the cross; but if we are joined together to be one *body*, we must have the cross. For the cross will take you and me away, it will take away our natural life, our individual movement, our inflated self. The cross is a must among Christians, it is a must in the church. Whether we like it or not, we must communicate with our brothers and sisters because we are all in the same body. Being in the body, we have to accept restraint. We cannot afford to be free-handed. Now if we do not wish to be a member of the body, we may indeed seek for our personal satisfaction alone. But if we want to be a member, we cannot look only for our own fulfillment. If you or I should encounter a troublesome brother, we really need the cross in such a situation. For the cross

will test us, the cross will drain out all our offscour-
ings, it will clear away all our uncleanness. In short,
we must be restrained by the body. Such restraint
makes impossible our freewheeling. It reminds us of
the need of the cross. Unless we allow the cross to do a
deep enough work in our lives we are not able to be
fitly joined to our brothers and sisters.

Because each Christian is a member of the body of
Christ he must accept its restraint and must learn to
bear the cross. Some members are highly individualistic; such strong individualism needs to be broken.
Some are quite offensively peculiar, and such peculiarity must also be broken. No Christian in the
church can boast of his toughness and peculiarity. In
the church, whatever is sharp, piercing, and protrud-
ing must be rubbed smooth.

In spiritual things how we need to depend on other
members and in so doing to know the restraint of the
body. Some members are given by God the gift of performing miracles; some receive grace to preach the
gospel; and others are divinely equipped to be teach-
ers. If you are chosen to preach the gospel, preach it
with glad and willing heart, and be humble enough to
receive the Bible teaching from those who are gifted
to teach. If you have the gift of a teacher, do not
therefore consider yourself as able in all other things.
You should respect and receive the gift and work of
others. In this, too, we need to learn restraint. What
we cannot do, we should let others do; and we should
learn to accept the work of other people as if it is our
own. In spiritual work, no one can do everything
freely.

Allow me to inquire of you, Have you asked God to show you what your measure is before Him? You should act according to the measure which God has apportioned to you. This is what you can do, and you must not stretch yourself beyond it. Find out your own measure and stay within that measure. If you accept the limitation of such measure you will not be tempted with greediness or some other ambition. In this regard, let us take note of what Paul said to the Corinthian believers: "According to the measure of the limit which God apportioned to us as a measure, [we] reach even to you. For we stretch not ourselves overmuch, as though we reached not unto you . . . but having hope that, as your faith groweth, we shall be magnified in you according to our limit unto further abundance, so as to preach the gospel even unto the parts beyond you, and not to glory in another's province in regard of things ready to our hand" (2 Cor. 10.13–16 mg.). To go beyond one's measure is to step on another's province. Going beyond one's measure is kicking and ousting others. Let us be aware of this, that our consecration should cause us to obey the body with humility as much as to obey Christ. "Neither do I exercise myself in great matters," declared King David, "or in things too wonderful for me" (Ps. 131.1). Those things which are great and too wonderful are matters which stretch a person beyond his measure. If all members of the body of Christ will keep to this rule—not daring to venture forth into areas which are too great and too wonderful for them—all will be able to work in the due measure of each several part, thus manifesting the functions of each member. Otherwise, some in the church will monopolize and some will draw back; with the result that the church will suffer loss. In view of this, let all believers return to their places in the body and accept its restraint so that the church may not incur any harm.

The Supply of the Body

The body possesses an inherent principle, which is fellowship. The fellowship of the body means not just receiving but also supplying. Should you only regard yourself as one on the receiving end of things and reckon yourself as fairly good if you receive with quietness and in an orderly manner, you lack an understanding of the meaning of the supply of the body. You also will become a weight to the body, an ailment and a burden to it.

Keep in mind that fellowship is the life of the church, that fellowship is an inherent principle of the body. Every part of our physical body is involved in a constant flow of life. Whenever a part is cut off from the body's system of communication, that part dies. But when a part is sick, all other parts of the body rush to help and to protect it. Now just as the law of the physical body is, so is the law of the spiritual body. The rule of church life, therefore, is the principle of mutual supplying. And whenever a member violates this rule, he brings death to the body and he himself becomes a weight upon it.

"What is it then, brethren? When ye come together, each one hath a psalm, hath a teaching, hath a revelation, hath a tongue, hath an interpretation. Let all things be done unto edifying" (1 Cor. 14.26). So Paul instructed the Corinthians believers. Some people come to a church meeting as if they were tourists or spectators. Coming in such a manner will doubtless bring death to the meeting. Many times death is felt in church meetings, a death which has been brought in by such visitors as these. Let this not be so. Let there be a mutual supplying of one another in all the meetings, not only in times of the breaking of bread but also in the hours of the ministry of the word of God.

Like the physical body, all the member parts of the spiritual body of Christ are incessantly communicating with each other: no part can stop at where it is. If any part should cease communicating, it stops the flow of the life of God and brings in death to the body. No member can stop communicating or fellowshiping without doing damage to the church, neither can any member be useful without the need of the supply of the church. Some believers, upon being provoked, tend to retreat to a place all by themselves. They assume that as long as they seek to be spiritual, everything will be all right. Well, you just try to grow spiritually by this method and see what will happen. It will not bear positive fruit, for life must constantly flow. Never imagine we can be spiritual by setting ourselves aside in isolation. And keep well in mind that the vessel which God ultimately seeks after is the body, not the individual. Whoever is isolated or separated from the church is not able to continue long.

On the day that the Lord Jesus sat down by the well of Jacob in Samaria He was hungry and thirsty.

But the Samaritan woman was more thirsty than the Lord. So He offered living water to her that she might be satisfied. When the disciples came back with the food, He was no longer hungry (see John 4.5–34). From this episode in the life of our Lord we learn this spiritual lesson, that whoever serves others in order that they may not be thirsty shall himself be satisfied: that the one who learns to bear another's burden shall find his own burden easier to bear. In spiritual work, there is no possibility of retirement: "My Father worketh even until now," declared the Lord Jesus, "and I work" (John 5.17). The Christians should therefore render the supply of life in their daily walk and work as well as in the meetings of the church.

May God open our eyes to see the body of Christ so that we may receive the covering and the restraint of the body as well as bring supply to others. May He cause us to see that everyone of us has a part to play in the meetings of the church. To utter the word "body" only with our lips is totally inadequate; the concept of "the body" must be in our hearts and manifested in our daily walk. For the body of Christ is not merely a teaching, it is an actual life to be lived. If you think you can live without the restraint, the protection, and the supply of the church, it is quite evident you have not received the revelation of the body of Christ. After you have received the life of God you will invariably feel dry if you live by your natural life. Similarly, after you have received the revelation concerning the body of Christ you will sense inadequacy if you live independently in your own self.

Without revelation on a given teaching, you will have to hold on tightly to the teaching lest you forget it. But once you have the revelation about it, it becomes quite natural to your life so that you have no further need to exercise yourself in trying to remember it. Take the example from the physical realm: your eyes wink without any need of remembrance and your eyes close and open automatically without mental recall. The same is true in the spiritual realm—for example, with respect to the body of Christ. With revelation given concerning the body, you sense in yourself the need to experience the body. You do not need to memorize it as a concept or a teaching or an external law and try to put it into practice. That which is done according to external law is Jewish in nature. And what is done through remembering a law is not life. If our interior realm has been touched by the Lord and our inner eyes have been opened to perceive what the body of Christ is, we will just naturally live in its reality.

Hence what is important here is the need for revelation. God wants to recover the life of the body, not the teaching of the body. The body of Christ is a life which needs to be experienced. We must enter into the reality of it. And if we live in the reality of the body of Christ we will know how concrete it is. We will not only understand its principles but we will also live out its life.

8 | Three Cardinal Principles On Living in the Body of Christ

We have been shown clearly in the previous chapters that in the body of Christ there are many members—and yet all these members are one, with each having its particular office or function; for God has not made all members the same but has made every member differently. This fact Paul has made plain in Romans 12: "For even as we have many members in one body, [yet] all the members have not the same office [function]" (v.4). But how, then, can all these members with their various functions be fitly framed and knit together as one body? This is the question for our present consideration here. In answering this question, we must first realize that there are three cardinal principles which are indispensable to our living in the body of Christ—the first of which governs the relationship between me and the head; the second of which governs the relationship between me and the body; and the third, my place as a member.

My Relation to the Head (Christ)—Subjection

The meaning of my Christian consecration has to

do with my desire to be obedient to the Lord. I do not want to be free, nor will I be rebellious to authority. The first principle on living in the body of Christ is to be in subjection to the authority of the head, since the very existence of the body with its varied functions and activities depend on authority. Whenever authority loses its ground in us, the body is immediately paralyzed. Whichever part of the body is disobedient, that part experiences paralysis. It is only a paralyzed body which is not subject to the command of the head. Where life is, there is authority. It is inconceivable to reject authority and still receive life.

All who are full of life have been obedient to authority. How, for example, can my physical hand have life and yet resist the control of my head? My hand is living because it is manageable by my head. The very meaning of living for my hand signifies that my head is able to direct and use it. The same is true in the relationship between any member of the body of Christ and the head. The very first principle for each member who lives in the body of Christ, therefore, is to obey the Lord who is the head. If you and I have not been dealt with until such time as we become obedient persons, then what we know about the body is merely doctrinal in nature, not a matter of life.

What a blessed thing it is to have God deal with our natural life, causing us to be in subjection to Christ the head! We ought to seek for obedience daily. Not only should we look for opportunities by which to advance spiritually that we may be holy and righteous, we should also seek before God every opportunity to obey that we may likewise learn obedience.

My Relation to the Body (Church)—Fellowship

Our relationship to the head is subjection, while our relationship to the body is fellowship. Among God's children, fellowship is not only a fact but also a necessity. The life of the body of Christ relies on fellowship, for without it the body will die. What is fellowship? For me to receive help from other members—that is fellowship. For example, in the body of Christ perhaps I am a mouth, and I can therefore speak forth. But I need the fellowship of that member who may be ears in order that I may also hear; I need the fellowship of him who may be eyes so that I may see; I require the fellowship of the one who may be hands in the body in order that I may take hold of things; and I also require the fellowship of the member who supplies feet to the body in order that I may walk. And hence it is by means of fellowship that I can receive the distinctive functions of other members and thus make all that they have mine.

Some Christians do not understand the principle of fellowship. They wish to seek the Lord by themselves and to pray by themselves. They themselves do all things. They want to be not only a mouth but also ears, to be hands as well as feet. Not so with those who know God, because they know they need fellowship. In fellowship they acknowledge that they themselves are limited and insufficient. Through fellowship they gladly receive as their own what the others have.

What is true of fellowship in the realm of teaching can be most real in fact. For can any of us honestly say that he has actually prayed three hundred sixty-

five days in the year or that he has carefully read the
Bible every day of the year ? Experience tells us that
due to physical weakness or some other cause we cannot avoid having a day or two in the year wherein we
are unable to pray and read the Bible as we should. Is
it because of such deficiency that I must therefore be
defeated? that I must fall to the ground? No, not at
all. For most surprisingly, within a given week, say on
Monday of that week, I may feel rather near to God,
and from Tuesday to Friday I continue to feel all
right, but that on Saturday I neither pray nor read the
Bible as I should—due probably to fatigue: yet I do not
necessarily fall on Saturday, nor need I be worse than
Friday; for strangely enough, a power seems to sustain
me and bring me through the day. Now what is the
cause for such support? Is it not due to the supply of
the life of the body?

Many of God's children can testify to this kind of
experience. And this happens not just once or twice,
but numerous times. According to our own condition
we are extremely weak, but God carries us through.
How? By means of the mutual supply of the body of
Christ. Unknown to others, some member in the body
is praying, asking God to give grace to all His children. And hence life flows from another member to
us, thus enabling us to stand. The life of the body is
able to flow into us and carry us through.

My Place As a Member—Service

If we have now seen that the life of the body is
communicative and mutually supplying, we should

likewise begin to realize before God that we should not be simply those who consume life but even more so be those who supply life. If there are too few members to supply life in the body of Christ while at the same time there are too many members who wait to receive the life supply, the strength of the body will be exhausted. Accordingly, we ourselves need to pray for other people. God will use our prayer to supply life to other members. Whenever they have need, life will flow into them.

"And whether one member suffereth, all the members suffer with it; or one member is honored, all the members rejoice with it" (1Cor. 12.26). It does not say here that if one member suffers, all the members *ought* to suffer with it; nor does it say if one member is honored, all the members *ought* to rejoice with it. The word of God does not say whether we ought to or not. On the contrary, God's word declares quite plainly that if one member suffers, all the other members *do in fact* suffer with it—and that if one member is honored, all the other members *do in actual fact* rejoice with it. This statement will therefore explain why frequently you and I may experience odd sensations. Often we do not understand why on a given occasion we feel so heavy and yet after two days the heaviness disappears. May I say that this is due to no other reason than the relationship which exists in the body of Christ among the various members.

Such a phenomenon can be illustrated by an occurrence which took place during the time of the great Welsh Revival. In one remote area a sister was praying one day with two or three other Christians. Oddly, on that day she felt the sweeping power of the Holy Spirit upon her. She had never had such an experience before. Such a condition continued on for four to five months, during which period she found it quite easy to touch God without the slightest effort—as though heaven itself had drawn very close to her. And this went on until one day, as she read the paper, she was shown by God that she had been wonderfully supplied by the Revival. This is exactly what the Scripture means by saying that if one member is honored all the other members rejoice with it. Let us realize this very thing, that the body of Christ is a living entity: it is an organic life. Said Paul: "I . . . fill up on my part that which is lacking of the afflictions of Christ in my flesh for his body's sake, which is the church" (Col. 1.24). Because we are in the one body, we can therefore fill up that which is lacking in the other members.

Hence this is not just a matter of suffering and rejoicing, it is a matter of life. Some people are able to supply life to the church; other people are able to receive life through the church. We must have this life flow in both directions. On the one side, we receive the supply of the body through fellowship; on the other side, we as members of the body supply life to others. Let us not apprehend the body merely as a teaching or a way of explanation. Let us see that the body of Christ is an absolute reality and that all the children of God being members one of another is likewise an irrefutable fact. And in view of these certainties, we should gladly receive help from others as well as earnestly seek to help other brothers and sisters.